*The Poems selected by
Claud Lovat Fraser.
This Edition is printed
by Harold Curwen,
at the Curwen Press,
Plaistow, and published
14 March, 1922*

Second Thousand

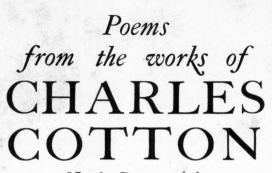

Poems
from the works of
CHARLES
COTTON

Newly Decorated by
CLAUD LOVAT FRASER

The Poetry Bookshop

35 *Devonshire Street*
Theobalds Road
London, W.C. 1

Note

CLAUD LOVAT FRASER made
his own selections from the Poems of
Charles Cotton, transcribing them
into a notebook and adding decora-
tions from time to time between other
work. This volume preserves in every
detail the artist's own selection and
arrangement.

Cotton's poems were a continual
pleasure to him, and he was always
trying to persuade his friends of their
rare qualities. He was in sympathy
both with their period and their style.
His seventy-five drawings were done
slowly and deliberately, and with the
greatest enjoyment. They represent
him at his best as a book-decorator
and as an artist.

Contents

Cælia's Fall

I

CÆLIA, my fairest Cælia, fell,
    Cælia, than the fairest, fairer,
    Cælia, (with none I must compare her)
    That all alone is all in all,
    Of what we fair and modest call,
    Cælia, white as Alabaster,
    Cælia, than Diana chaster,
This fair, fair Cælia, greif to tell,
This fair, this modest, chast one fell.

II

My Cælia, sweetest Cælia, fell,
    As I have seen a Snow-white Dove
    Decline her Bosom from above,
    And down her spotless body fling,
    Without the motion of the wing,
    Till she arrest her seeming fall,
    Upon some happy Pedestal:
So soft this sweet, I love so well,
This sweet, this Dovelike Cælia fell.

III

Cælia, my dearest Cælia, fell,
　　As I have seen a melting Star
　　Drop down its fire from its Sphear,
　　Rescuing so its glorious sight
　　From that paler snuff of Light:
　　Yet is a Star bright and entire,
　　As when 'twas wrapt in all that fire:
So bright, this dear, I love so well,
This dear, this Starlike Cælia fell.

IV

And yet my Cælia did not fall
　　As grosser Earthly Mortals do,
　　But stooped, like Phœbus, to renew
　　Her lustre by her Morning rise,
　　And dart new Beauties in the Skies.
　　Like a White Dove, she took her flight,
　　And like a Star, she shot her Light.
This Dove, this Star, so lov'd of all,
My Fair, Dear, Sweetest, did not fall.

V

But if you'll say my Cælia fell,
　　Of this I'm sure, that, like the Dart
　　Of Love it was, and on my Heart;
　　Poor Heart, alas! wounded before,
　　She needed not have hurt it more:
　　So absolute a Conquest she
　　Had gain'd before of it, and me,
That neither of us have been well
Before, or since my Cælia fell.

Resolution in Four Sonnets of a Poetical
Question put to me by a Friend concerning
Four Rural Sisters

FIRST SONNET

ALICE is tall and upright as a Pine,
White as blaunch'd Almonds or the falling Snow,
Sweet as are Damask Roses when they blow,
And doubtless fruitful as the swelling Vine.

Ripe to be cut, and ready to be press'd,
Her full-cheek'd beauties very well appear,
And a year's fruit she loses ev'ry year,
Wanting a man t' improve her to the best.

Full fain she would be husbanded, and yet,
Alas! she cannot a fit Lab'rer get
To cultivate her to her own content:

Fain would she be (God wot) about her task,
And yet (forsooth) she is too proud to ask,
And (which is worse) too modest to consent.

SECOND SONNET

MARG'RET of humbler stature by the head
Is (as it oft falls out with yellow hair)
Than her fair Sister, yet so much more fair,
As her pure white is better mixt with red.

This, hotter than the other ten to one,
Longs to be put unto her Mother's trade,
And loud proclaims she lives too long a Maid,
Wishing for one t' untie her Virgin Zone.

She finds Virginity a kind of ware
That's very very troublesome to bear,
And being gone, she thinks will ne'er be mist.

And yet withall the Girl has so much grace,
To call for help I know she wants the face,
Though ask't, I know not how she would resist.

THIRD SONNET

MARY is black, and taller than the last,
Yet equal in perfection and desire,
To the one's melting snow and t' other's fire,
As with whose black their fairness is defac'd:

She pants as much for love as th' other two,
But she so vertuous is or else so wise,
That she will win or will not love a prize,
And but upon good terms will never doe:

Therefore who her will conquer ought to be
At least as full of love and wit as she,
Or he shall ne'er gain favour at her hands:

Nay, though he have a pretty store of brains,
Shall only have his labour for his pains,
Unless he offer more than she demands.

FOURTH SONNET

MARTHA is not so tall, nor yet so fair
As any of the other lovely three,
Her chiefest Grace is poor Simplicity,
Yet were the rest away, she were a Star.

She's fair enough, only she wants the Art
To set her Beauties off as they can doe,
And that's the cause she ne'er heard any woo,
Nor ever yet made conquest of a heart:

And yet her bloud's as boiling as the best,
Which, pretty soul, does so disturb her rest,
And makes her languish so, she's fit to die.

Poor thing, I doubt she still must lie alone,
For, being like to be attacked by none,
Sh'as no more wit to ask than to deny.

A Sonnet

CHLORIS, whilst thou and I were free,
Wedded to naught but Liberty,
How sweetly happy did we live?
How free to promise, free to give?

Then Monarchs of ourselves, we might
Love here, or there, to change delight,
And, ty'd to none, with all dispence,
Paying each Love its recompence.

But in that happy freedom we
Were so improvidently free
   To give away our Liberties:

And now in fruitless Sorrow pine
At what we are, what might have been,
   Had thou, or I, or both been wise.

EPITAPH
On Mr. ROBERT PORT

HERE lies he whom the Tyrant's rage
Snatch't in a venerable Age;
And here, with him, intomb'd do lie
Honour, and Hospitality.

Summer
Quatrains:
Morning, Noon, Evening
Night

Morning Quatrains

I

THE Cock has crow'd an hour ago,
'Tis time we now dull sleep forgo;
Tir'd Nature is by sleep redress'd,
And Labour's overcome by Rest.

We have outdone the work of Night,
'Tis time we rise t' attend the Light,
And e'er he shall his Beams display,
To plot new bus'ness for the day.

None but the slothfull, or unsound,
Are by the Sun in Feathers found,
Nor, without rising with the Sun,
Can the World's bus'ness e'er be done.

Hark! Hark! the watchfull Chanticler,
Tells us the day's bright Harbinger
Peeps o'er the Eastern Hills, to awe
And warn Night's Sov'reign to withdraw.

The Morning Curtains now are drawn,
And now appears the blushing dawn;
Aurora has her Roses shed,
To strew the way Sol's steeds must tread.

Xanthus and Æthon harness'd are,
To roll away the burning Carr,
And, snorting flame, impatient bear
The dressing of the Chariotier.

The sable cheeks of Sullen Night
Are streak'd with Rosie streams of light,
Whilst she retires away in fear,
To shade the other Hemisphere.

The merry Lark now takes her wings,
And long'd-for days loud wellcome sings,
Mounting her body out of sight,
As if she meant to meet the Light.

Now doors and windows are unbar'd,
Each-where are chearfull voices heard,
And round about Good-morrows fly,
As if Day taught Humanity.

The Chimnies now to smoke begin
And the old Wife sits down to spin,
Whilst Kate, taking her Pail, does trip
Mull's swoln and stradling Paps to strip.

Vulcan now makes his Anvil ring,
Dick whistles loud, and Maud doth sing,
And Silvio, with his Bugle-Horn,
Winds an Imprime unto the Morn.

Now through the morning doors behold
Phœbus array'd in burning Gold,
Lashing his fiery Steeds, displays
His warm and all-enlight'ning Rays.

Now each one to his work prepares,
All that have hands are Labourers,
And Manufactures of each trade
By op'ning Shops are open laid.

Hob yokes his Oxen to the Team,
The Angler goes unto the stream,
The Woodman to the Purlews highs,
And lab'ring Bees to load their thighs.

Fair Amarillis drives her Flocks,
All night safe folded from the Fox,
To flow'ry Downs, where Collin stays,
To court her with his Roundelays.

The Traveller now leaves his Inn,
A new day's Journey to begin,
As he would post it with the day,
And early rising makes good way.

The slick-fac'd School-boy Sachel takes,
And with slow pace small riddance makes;
For why? The haste we make, you know,
To Knowledge and to Vertue's slow.

The Fore-horse gingles on the Road,
The Waggoner lugs on his Load,
The Field with Busy People snies,
And City rings with various cries.

The world is now a busie swarm,
All doing good, or doing harm;
But let's take heed our Acts be true,
For Heaven's eye sees all we doe.

23

None can that piercing sight evade,
It penetrates the darkest shade,
And sin, though it should 'scape the eye,
Would be discover'd by the cry.

Noon Quatrains

THE day grows hot, and darts his Rays
From such a sure and killing place,
That this half World are fain to fly
The danger of his burning eye.

His early Glories were benign,
Warm to be felt, bright to be seen,
And all was comfort; but who can
Endure him when Meridian?

Of him we as of Kings complain,
Who mildly do begin to reign,
But to the Zenith got of pow'r,
Those whom they should protect devour.

Has not another Phaeton
Mounted the Chariot of the Sun,
And, wanting Art to guide his Horse,
Is hurri'd from the Sun's due course.

If this hold on, our fertile Lands
Will soon be turn'd to parched Sands,
And not an Onion that will grow
Without a Nile to overflow.

The grazing Herds now droop and pant,
E'en without labour fit to faint,
And willingly forsook their Meat
To seek out cover from the heat.

The lagging Ox is now unbound,
From larding the new turn'd-up ground,
Whilst Hobbinal alike o'er-laid,
Takes his course dinner to the shade.

Cellars and Grottos now are best
To eat and drink in, or to rest,
And not a Soul above is found
Can find a refuge under ground.

When Pagan Tyranny grew hot,
Thus persecuted Christians got
In to the dark but friendly Womb
Of unknown Subterranean Rome.

And as that heat did cool at last,
So a few scorching hours o'er pass'd,
In a more mild and temp'rate Ray
We may again enjoy the day.

Evening Quatrains

THE Day's grown old, the fainting Sun
Has but a little way to run,
And yet his Steeds, with all his skill,
Scarce lug the Chariot down the Hill.

With Labour spent, and Thirst opprest,
Whilst they strain hard to gain the West,
From Fetlocks hot drops melted light,
Which turn to Meteors in the Night.

The Shadows now so long do grow,
That Brambles like tall Cedars show,
Mole-hills seem Mountains, and the Ant
Appears a monstrous Elephant.

A very little little Flock
Shades thrice the ground that it would stock;
Whilst the small Stripling following them,
Appears a mighty Polypheme.

These being brought into the Fold,
And by the thrifty Master told,
He thinks his Wages are well paid,
Since none are either lost, or stray'd.

Now lowing Herds are each-where heard,
Chains rattle in the Villain's Yard,
The Carts on Tayl set down to rest,
Bearing on high the Cuckold's Crest.

The hedge is stript, the Clothes brought in,
Nought's left without should be within,
The Bees are hiv'd and hum their Charm,
Whilst every House does seem a Swarm.

The Cock now to the Roost is prest:
For he must call up all the rest;
The Sow's fast pegg'd within the Sty,
To still her squeaking Progeny.

Each one has had his Supping Mess,
The Cheese is put into the Press,
The Pans and Bowls clean scalded all,
Rear'd up against the Milk-house wall.

And now on Benches all are sat
In the cool Air to sit and chat,
Till Phœbus, dipping in the West,
Shall lead the World the way to Rest.

Night Quatrains

THE Sun is set, and gone to sleep
With the fair Princess of the Deep,
Whose Bosom is his cool Retreat,
When fainting with his proper Heat:

His Steeds their flaming Nostrils cool
In spume of the Cerulean Pool;
Whilst the Wheels dip their hissing Naves
Deep in Columbus's Western Waves.

From whence great rowls of Smoke arise
To overshade the Beauteous Skies:
Who bid the World's bright Eye adieu
In gelid tears of falling Dew.

And now from the Iberian Vales
Night's sable Steeds her Chariot hales,
Where double Cypress Curtains skreen
The gloomy Melancholick Queen.

These, as they higher mount the Sky,
Ravish all Colour from the Eye,
And leave it but an useless glass,
Which few, or no Reflections grace.

The Crystal Arch o're Pindus's Crown
Is on a sudden dusky grown,
And all's with Fun'ral Black o're spread,
As if the Day, which sleeps, were dead.

No Ray of Light the Heart to chear,
But little twinkling Stars appear;
Which like faint dying Embers ly,
Fit not to work, nor travel by.

Perhaps to him they Torches are,
Who guide Night's Sovereign's drowsy Car,
And him they may befriend so near,
But us they neither Light, nor chear.

Or else those little sparks of light
Are Nayls that tyre the Wheels of Night,
Which to new stations still are brought,
As they rowl o'r the gloomy Vault.

Or Nayls that arm the Horse's hoof,
Which trampling o're the marble Roof,
And striking Fire in the Air,
We Mortals call a shooting Star.

That's all the Light we now receive,
Unless what belching Vulcans give,
And those yield such a kind of Light
As adds more horror to the Night.

Nyctimine now freed from day,
From sullen Bush flies out to prey,
And does with Feret note proclaim
Th' arrival of th' usurping Dame.

The Rail now cracks in Fields and Meads,
Toads now forsake the Nettle-beds,
The tim'rous Hare goes to relief,
And wary men bolt out the Theef.

The Fire's new rak't, and Hearth swept clean,
By Madg, the dirty Kitchin-Quean;
The Safe is lock't, the Mouse-trap set,
The Leaven laid, and Bucking wet.

Now in false Floors and Roofs above,
The lustful Cats make ill-tun'd Love,
The Ban-dog on the Dunghil lies,
And watchful Nurse sings Lullabies.

Philomel chants it whilst she bleeds,
The Bittern booms it in the Reeds,
And Reynard ent'ring the back Yard,
The Capitolian Cry is heard.

The Goblin now the Fool alarms,
Haggs meet to mumble o're their Charms;
The Night-mare rides the dreaming Ass,
And Fairies trip it on the grass.

The Drunkard now supinely snores,
His load of Ale sweats through his Pores,
Yet when he wakes the Swine shall find
A Cropala remains behind.

The Sober now and Chast are blest
With sweet, and with refreshing rest,
And to sound sleeps they've best pretence,
Have greatest share of Innocence.

We should so live then that we may
Fearless put off our Clotts and Clay,
And travel through Death's shades to Light;
For every Day must have its Night.

Here end
the Quatrains

Epigram de Mons. Maynard

ANTHONY feigns him Sick of late,
  Only to shew how he at home,
Lies in a Princely Bed of State,
  And in a nobly furnish'd Room,
    Adorn'd with Pictures of Vandike's,
    A pair of Chrystal Candlesticks,
      Rich Carpets, Quilts, the Devil, and all:
    Then you, his careful Friends, if ever
    You wish to cure him of his Fever,
      Go lodge him in the Hospital.

Sonnet

WHAT have I left to doe but dye,
Since Hope, my old Companion,
That train'd me from my Infancy,
My Friend, my Comforter is gone?

Oh fawning, false, deceiving Friend!
Accursed be thy Flatteries,
Which treacherously did intend
I should be wretched to be wise:

And so I am; for being taught
To know thy guiles, have only wrought
  My greater misery and pain:

My misery is yet so great,
That, though I have found out the Cheat,
  I wish for thee again in vain.

Winter

HARK, hark, I hear the North Wind roar,
See how he riots on the Shoar;
And, with expanded Wings at stretch,
Ruffels the Billows on the Beach.

Hark how the routed Waves complain,
And call for Succor to the Main,
Flying the Storm as if they meant
To creep into the Continent.

Surely all Æoll's huffing Brood
Are met to War against the Flood,
Which seem surpris'd, and have not yet
Had time his Levies to compleat.

The beaten Bark her Rudder lost,
Is on the rowling Billows tost;
Her Keel now plows the Ouse, and soon
Her Top-Mast tillts against the Moon.

'Tis strange! the Pilot keeps his seat;
His bounding Ship does so curvet,
Whilst the poor Passengers are found,
In their own fears already drown'd.

Now Fins do serve for Wings, and bear
Their Scaly Squadrons through the Air;
Whilst the Air's Inhabitants do stain
Their gaudy Plumage in the Main.

Now Stars concealed in Clouds do peep
Into the Secrets of the deep;
And Lobsters spued from the brine
With Cancer constellations shine.

Sure Neptune's Watery Kingdoms yet
Since first their Corral Graves were wet,
Were ne're disturbed with such alarms,
Nor had such trial of their Arms.

See where a Liquid Mountain rides,
Made up of innumerable Tides,
And tumbles headlong to the Strand,
As if the Sea would come to Land.

A Sail, a Sail, I plainly spy
Betwixt the Ocean and the Sky,
An Argosy, a tall built Ship,
With all her Pregnant Sails a-trip.

Nearer, and nearer, she makes way,
With Canvis Wings into the Bay;
And now upon the Deck appears
A croud of busy Mariners.

Methinks I hear the Cordage crack,
With furrowing Neptune's foaming Back,
Who wounded, and revengeful roars
His fury to the neighb'ring Shoars.

With massy Trident high, he heaves
Her sliding Keel above the Waves,
Opening his Liquid Arms to take
The bold invader in his wrack.

See how she dives into his Chest,
Whilst raising up his floating Brest
To clasp her in, he makes her rise
Out of the reach of his surprise.

Nearer she comes, and still doth sweep
The Azure Surface of the deep,
And now at last the Waves have thrown
Their Rider on our ALBION

Under the Black cliff, spumy base,
The Sea-sick Hulk her fraight displays,
And as she walloweth on the Sand
Vomits her burthen to the Land.

With Heads erect, and plying Oar,
The ship-wracked Mates make to the Shoar;
And dreadless of their danger, climb
The floating Mountains of the brine.

Hark, hark, the noise their Eccho make
The Islands Silver Waves to shake;
Sure with these throws, the lab'ring Main
'S delivered of a Hurricane.

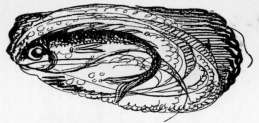

And see the Sea's becalm'd behind,
Not crispt with any breeze of Wind;
The Tempest has forsook the Waves,
And on the Land begins his braves.

Hark, hark their Voices higher rise,
They tear the Welkin with their Cries;
The very Rocks their fury feel,
And like sick Drunkards nod, and reel.

Louder, and louder, still they come,
Nile's Cataracts to these are dumb;
The Cyclope to these Blades are still,
Whose Anvils shake the burning Hill.

Were all the Stars enlight'ned Skies,
As full of Ears as sparkling Eyes;
This rattle on the Chrystal Hall
Would be enough to deaf them all.

What monstrous Race is hither tost
Thus to Alarm our British Coast;
With Outcries such as never yet
War or Confusion could beget.

Oh! now I know them Let us home:
Our Mortal Enemy is come,
Winter and all his blust'ring train
Have made a voyage o'er the Main.

Vanish't the Countrys of the Sun,
The Fugitive is hither run,
To ravish from our fruitful Fields
All that the teeming Season Yields.

Like an Invader, not a Guest,
He comes to Riot, not to Feast;
And in wild fury overthrows
Whatever does his march oppose.

With bleak and with congealing Winds,
The Earth in shining Chains he binds;
And still as he doth farther pass,
Quarries his way with Liquid Glass.

Hark ! how the Blusterors of the Bear,
Their Gibbouse Cheeks in Triumph tear,
And with continued Shouts do ring
The entry of their Palsy'd King.

The Squadron nearest to your Eye
Is his Forlorn of Infantry,
Bowmen of unrelenting Minds,
Whose Shafts are Feathered with the Winds.

Now you may see his Van-guard rise
Above the Earthy Precipice,
Bold Horse on bleakest Mountains bred,
With Hail instead of Provend fed.

Their Launces are the pointed Locks
Torn from the Brows of Frozen Rocks,
Their Shields are Chrystals as their Swords,
The steel the rusted Rock affords.

See the main Body now appears,
And hark the Aeolian Trumpetters
By their Hoarse Levets do declare
That the bold General rides there.

And look when Mantled up in white,
He steads it like the Muscovite:
I know him by the Port he bears
And his Life-guard of Mountaineers.

Their Caps are Fur'd with Hoary Frost,
The Bravery their Cold Kingdom boasts:
Their spungy Plads are Milk-white Frieze,
Spun from the Snowy Mountain's Fleece.

Their Partizans are fine carved Glass
Fringed with the Mornings spangled Grass;
And, Pendant by their brawny Thighs,
Hang Cimetars of burnisht Ice.

See, see, the Reerward now has won
The Promontories trembling Crown,
Whilst at their numerous Spurs, the Ground
Groans out a hollow murmering Sound.

The Forlorn now halts for the Van;
The Reer-guard draws up to the Main;
And now they altogether crowd
Their Troops into a threat'ning Cloud.

Fly, Fly; the foe advances fast
Into our Fortress, let us hast
Where all the Roarers of the North
Can neither Storm, nor Starve us forth.

There under Ground a Magazine
Of Sovereign juice is collard in,
Liquor that will the Seige maintain
Shou'd Phoebus ne'er return again.

Till that, that gives the Poet rage,
And thaws the gelly'd Blood of Age;
Matures the Young, restores the Old,
And makes the fainting Coward bold.

It lays the careful Head to rest,
Calms Palpitations in the Breast,
Renders our Lives misfortune Sweet,
And Venus frolick in the Sheet.

Then let the chill Sciorocco blow,
And gird us round with Hills of Snow;
Or else go whistle to the Shoar,
And make the hollow Mountains roar.

Whilst we together jovial sit
Careless and Crown'd with Mirth and Wit;
Where, though bleak Winds confine us Home,
Our fancies round the World shall roam.

We'll think of all the Friends we know,
And Drink to all worth Drinking to:
When having Drunk all thine and mine,
We rather shall want Health than Wine.

But where Friends fail us, we'll supply
Our friendships with our Charity:
Men that remote in Sorrows live
Shall by our lusty Brimmers thrive.

We'll Drink the Wanting into Wealth,
And those that Languish into Health,
The Afflicted into Joy, th' Opprest
Into Security and Rest.

The Worthy in Disgrace shall find
Favour return again more kind,
And in restraint who stifled lye
Shall taste the Air of Liberty.

The Brave shall triumph in Success,
The Lovers shall have Mistresses,
Poor unreguarded Virtue Praise,
And the Neglected Poet Baies.

Thus shall our Healths do others good,
Whilst we our selves do all we wou'd;
For, freed from Envy and from Care,
What would we be but what we are?

'Tis the plump Grapes Immortal Juice
That does this happiness produce,
And will preserve us free together,
Maugre mischance, or Wind and Weather.

Then let Old Winter take his course,
And roar abroad till he be hoarse,
And his Lungs crack with Ruthless Ire,
It shall but serve to blow our Fire.

Let him our little Castle ply
With all his loud Artillery,
Whilst Sack and Claret Man the Fort,
His Fury shall become our Sport.

Or, let him Scotland take, and there
Confine the plotting Presbyter;
His Zeal may Freeze, whilst we, kept warm
With Love and Wine, can know no harm.

Finis